FOOTBALL

Trace Taylor

CEDAR ISLAND ELEMENTARY SCHOOL
8777 Hemlock Lane North
Maple Grove, MN 55369

This is my shirt.

Here are my pants.

This is my helmet.

"You will like this one."

Here are my pads.

Here are my shoes.

This is my ball.

Here is my kick.

This is my catch.

Here is my bench.

This is my touchdown.

Here is my trophy.